Acting Out Jesus' Parables

A 4-week course to help teenagers use dramatic representations to explore and understand Jesus' parables

by Stephen Parolini

Group

Loveland, Colorado

Group

Acting Out Jesus' Parables
Copyright © 1994 Group Publishing, Inc.

Credits
Edited by Lois Keffer and Joani Schultz
Cover designed by Liz Howe and Amy Bryant
Title designed by Diana Walters
Illustrations by Randall Kady

11 10 9 8 7 6 5 4 3 2   04 03 02 01 00 99 98 97 96 95
ISBN 1-55945-147-5
Printed in the United States of America.

CONTENTS

Acting Out Jesus' Parables

Lesson 1   9

Planning the Project

Students will learn the purpose for this course and plan how they'll explore and act out Jesus' parables.

Lesson 2   19

Lifestyle Parables

Students will explore parables that describe the Christian lifestyle and plan dramatic representations of those parables.

Lesson 3   25

Kingdom Parables—Part One

Students will explore parables about God's kingdom and plan dramatic representations of those parables.

Lesson 4   31

Kingdom Parables—Part Two

Students will explore parables about God's kingdom and plan dramatic representations of those parables.

Introduction
ACTING OUT JESUS' PARABLES

When Jesus taught his disciples with parables, the disciples often came away confused. They didn't understand what Jesus was teaching and sometimes wished that he'd spoken in clear terms rather than veiling his teaching in analogies.

But Jesus knew that his disciples would learn more from "struggling" to understand parables than from simply ingesting straightforward statements about the kingdom of God or how Christians should live.

In many of today's schools, kids are taught to regurgitate correct answers, not to think for themselves. Instead of developing thinking skills of their own, kids often learn to give the answer the teacher wants to hear. Then, when kids face a difficult decision, they aren't equipped to make an intelligent choice.

Parables are great teaching tools because they require the hearers to think about what it means to be a Christian. Jesus' parables bring to light many issues of importance to young Christians—the value of humility, the importance of hope, and the relative unimportance of wealth.

But how should we study Jesus' parables?

It would be simple to open a Bible and have teenagers read the parables, then discuss them. And kids *will* do that in this course. But why stop there? By giving young people a project to work on—creating visual parables for the whole church to see—kids will learn much more about what the parables mean.

This course is designed to get teenagers talking about the parables. By studying the parables, discussing how they apply to kids' lives today, and preparing a living representation of what the parables mean, kids will create memories they won't soon forget. And memorable lessons are what this curriculum is all about.

Use **Acting Out Jesus' Parables** to get your young people excited about understanding Jesus' parables. Then, in a few years when you see the kids again, ask what they remember. You'll be surprised at how much of an impact this course can have.

And you'll be pleased that your students remember what you explored together during these four weeks.

COURSE OBJECTIVES

By the end of this course, your students will
- know what a parable is,
- determine what Jesus' parables mean for them today,

- create visual parables,
- learn how to apply Jesus' teachings to their lives, and
- act out parables for the rest of the church.

THIS COURSE AT A GLANCE

Before you dive into the lessons, familiarize yourself with each lesson aim. Then read the Scripture passages.
- Study them as a background to the lessons.
- Use them as a basis for your personal devotions.
- Think about how they relate to kids' circumstances today.

Lesson 1: PLANNING THE PROJECT
Lesson Aim: Students will learn the purpose for this course and plan how they'll explore and act out Jesus' parables.
Bible Basis: Matthew 13:1-23.

Lesson 2: LIFESTYLE PARABLES
Lesson Aim: Students will explore parables that describe the Christian lifestyle and plan dramatic representations of those parables.
Bible Basis: Luke 10:25-37; Luke 14:16-24; Luke 18:1-14; and Luke 19:12-27.

Lesson 3: KINGDOM PARABLES—PART ONE
Lesson Aim: Students will explore parables about God's kingdom and plan dramatic representations of those parables.
Bible Basis: Matthew 13:31-46 and Matthew 20:1-16.

Lesson 4: KINGDOM PARABLES—PART TWO
Lesson Aim: Students will explore parables about God's kingdom and plan dramatic representations of those parables.
Bible Basis: Matthew 13:24-30; Matthew 13:47-50; and Matthew 25:1-13.

HOW TO USE THIS COURSE

PROJECTS WITH A PURPOSE™ for Youth Ministry

Think back on an important lesson you've learned in life. Did you learn it by reading about it? from hearing a lecture about it?

Chances are, the most important lessons you've learned came from something you experienced. That's what active learning is—learning by doing. And active learning is a key element in Group's new Projects With a Purpose™ for Youth Ministry courses.

Active learning leads students in doing things that help them understand important principles, messages, and ideas. It's a discovery process that helps kids internalize what they learn.

Research about active learning indicates that maximum learning results when students are involved in direct, purposeful experiences. With that in mind, each Projects With a Purpose for Youth Ministry course gives teachers tools to facilitate some sort of project that results in direct, purposeful experiences for teenagers. Projects, experiences, and immersion in real-life faith in action characterize this curriculum. Each course produces a tangible result. You'll find plenty of helpful hints that'll make this course easy for you to teach and meaningful to your students.

Projects With a Purpose for Youth Ministry takes learning to a new level—giving teenagers an opportunity to discover something significant about their faith. And kids learn the important skills of working together, sharing one another's troubles, and supporting one another in love.

Projects With a Purpose for Youth Ministry offers a fun, alternative way for teenagers to put their faith into action. Use it today to involve your kids in Christian growth experiences they'll remember for a lifetime.

Before the 4-Week Course

■ Read the Introduction, the Course Objectives, and This Course at a Glance.

■ Determine when you'll use this course. Projects With a Purpose for Youth Ministry works well in Sunday school classes, midweek meetings, home Bible studies, confirmation classes, youth groups, special-interest groups, leadership groups, retreats, camps, or any time you want to help teenagers discover more about their faith.

■ Decide how you'll publicize the course using the clip art on the Publicity Page (p. 8). Prepare fliers, newsletter articles, and posters as needed.

■ Look at the Bonus Ideas (p. 37) and decide which ones you'll use.

Before Each Lesson

Read the opening statements, Objectives, and Bible Basis for the lesson. The Bible Basis focuses on a key biblical theme for the activity, experience, or Bible study portion of the lesson.

Gather necessary supplies from This Lesson at a Glance.

Read each section of the lesson. Adjust as necessary for your class size and meeting room.

Helpful Hints

■ The approximate minutes listed give you an idea of how long each activity will take. Each lesson in a Projects With a Purpose for Youth Ministry course is designed to fill an hourlong time slot. Some lessons may require work outside of class, depending on the project for the course. You might also consider restructuring your class time, if possible, to allow more time to complete projects.

> The answers given after discussion questions are responses your students *might* give. They aren't the only answers or the "right" answers. If needed, use them to spark discussion. Kids won't always say what you wish they'd say. That's why some of the responses given are negative or controversial. If someone responds negatively, don't be shocked. Accept the person and use the opportunity to explore other angles of the issue.

■ If you see you're going to have extra time, do an activity or two from the "If You Still Have Time..." section at the end of each lesson or from the Bonus Ideas (p. 37).

■ Dive into the activities with the kids. Don't be a spectator. The experience will be more successful and rewarding for both you and your students when you play an active role.

■ Have fun with the lessons as you lead your teenagers. Remember, it is Jesus who encourages us to become "like little children." Besides, how often do your kids get *permission* to express their childlike qualities?

■ Be prepared for surprises. In Projects With a Purpose for Youth Ministry lessons, you don't always know which way the lesson will go. Much of your job will be directing kids to stay on task rather than leading specific activities. As facilitator, you'll be helping kids make their own faith discoveries rather than directing the results of a specific activity.

■ Encourage new leaders to participate in teaching this course. Projects With a Purpose for Youth Ministry offers an exciting way to give new volunteers a hands-on look at the positive impact youth ministry can have on teenagers.

■ Rely on the Holy Spirit to help you. Remember, only God can give true spiritual insight. Concentrate on your role as the facilitator and trust the Holy Spirit to work in the hearts of your kids.

You Can Do It!

Because Projects With a Purpose for Youth Ministry is a different approach to Christian education, leading the lessons might seem a bit scary at first.

That's OK. In fact, it's normal to be a little nervous about a new teaching method. Innovation often requires a risk for the teacher. But hang in there. With the Holy Spirit's guidance and your own desire to make these lessons succeed, great things will happen in your kids' lives.

PUBLICITY PAGE

Grab your young people's attention! Photocopy this page, then cut out and paste the clip art of your choice in your church bulletin or newsletter to advertise this course on Jesus' parables. Or photocopy and use the ready-made flier as a bulletin insert. Permission to photocopy this clip art is granted for local church use.

Splash the clip art on posters, fliers, or even postcards! Just add the vital details: the date and time the course begins and where you'll meet.

It's that simple.

A 4-week youth course
on Jesus' parables

Come to ....

On ....

At ....

Join the adventure as we uncover the meaning of Jesus' parables through creative experiences.

Planning the Project

When Jesus taught his disciples with a parable, the disciples strived (and often struggled) to grasp the parable's meaning. Struggling to understand thought-provoking parables probably helped the disciples grow even more.

Young people today can also benefit from striving to understand what Jesus meant in his parables. This lesson will help kids begin to explore Jesus' parables and what they mean for us today.

Students will learn the purpose for this course and plan how they'll explore and act out Jesus' parables.

LESSON AIM

Students will
- define a parable,
- plan ways to live out the parables in the coming weeks,
- determine what Jesus' parables mean for us today, and
- create dramatic parables based on Matthew 13:3-9.

OBJECTIVES

Look up the following key Bible passage. Then read the background paragraphs to see how the passage relates to your young people. This Scripture will be explored during the Bible study portion of today's lesson.

BIBLE BASIS

MATTHEW 13:1-23

In **Matthew 13:1-23**, Jesus tells the parable of the sower and describes why he teaches with parables.

At first glance Jesus seems to be saying that he teaches in parables deliberately to confuse people. But upon further study, we see that Jesus taught with parables for other reasons.

First, parables were a common teaching method of Jesus' time. It was natural for Jesus to use a method familiar to people of his day.

Second, and more importantly, Jesus taught with parables to force the listeners to think and to search for "nuggets" of spiritual truth. Jesus knew that not everyone would dive into the parables to understand them. But he also knew that those who did wrestle with difficult-to-understand parables would find life-changing truths.

By showing teenagers why Jesus taught with parables, we can help them understand the importance of searching for the truth. Through this lesson young people will begin to explore the meaning of the parable of the sower.

Section	Minutes	What Students Will Do	Supplies
Introduction	5 to 10	**What's a Parable?**—Learn what today's lesson is about and discuss what a parable is.	
Bible Study	10 to 15	**Tough Thinking**—Read Matthew 13:10-17 and explore why Jesus taught with parables.	Bibles
Project Work	20 to 25	**Parable Beginning**—Learn the process for creating dramatic parables and begin work on their first dramatic parable.	Poster supplies, Bibles, "Dramatic-Parable Process" handouts (p. 16), pencils
	10 to 15	**Preparing the Teaser**—Plan advertisements for the upcoming dramatic parables.	Poster supplies, "Preparing the Teaser" handouts (p. 17), pencils
	5 to 10	**Parable Review**—Briefly review the message in today's parable.	
Closing	up to 5	**Thanks for Insight**—Thank God for the ability to uncover truths in Jesus' parables.	

BEFORE YOU BEGIN...

The Lesson

During the coming weeks your young people will prepare and perform dramatic parables for the whole church to see. A dramatic parable is a human sculpture or skit illustrating one of Jesus' parables.

Each week kids will prepare a teaser about the coming week's dramatic parable. The teaser will come in many different forms and will encourage congregation members to look for the parable during the coming week.

Parables may be performed in the church narthex, sanctuary, parking lot, or Christian education hall. The teaser will help adults know where to look for the young people doing the parable.

This course works whether you're meeting before or after worship, or a different day and time altogether. Notes for each scenario are included in the "Preparing the Teaser" section of each lesson.

If you're leading this course outside of regular church-school hours, remind kids they may be needed before, during, or after worship, depending on the parables being presented and how they'll act them out.

What's a Parable?

(5 to 10 minutes)

Welcome students to class. Say: **Today we're going to begin a four-week exploration of Jesus' parables. But we're not just going to read about parables—we're going to live them out for the whole church to see in what we'll call "dramatic parables."**

Open with prayer. Then ask:

■ **What is a parable?** (A story with a hidden meaning; a story that teaches a truth.)

Help kids clarify the meaning of the word "parable" by reading the following definition (or your own paraphrase of this definition): **A parable is a figure of speech in which a spiritual truth (or moral) is illustrated by something drawn from everyday experience.**

Say: **Many of Jesus' parables helped Jesus' followers understand what the kingdom of God was all about. Other parables taught about how to make good lifestyle choices. We'll explore both types of parables in the coming weeks. But before we begin, let's take a few minutes to get to know each other better.**

Have kids each complete the following analogy: **When it comes to everyday life, I'm most like...** Encourage kids to complete the statement by using a familiar occupation that describes them best. For example, someone might say "I'm most like someone who washes cars for a living" or "I'm most like an actor." Go around the group, but don't have kids explain their analogies. Remind kids to remember their analogies because you'll refer to them in the Bible study.

After each person has spoken, ask:

■ **What was it like to think of an analogy in this activity?** (Fun; it was easy; I couldn't think of one.)

■ **How is this simple activity like or unlike the way Jesus used parables when teaching the disciples?** (Jesus compared everyday things to spiritual truths; Jesus confused people, too.)

Say: **In some ways our analogies are similar to Jesus' parables. They used common experiences or, in this case, occupations to describe something else—who we are. Also, you may not have fully understood why people said what they did. Jesus' followers didn't always understand his parables, either. Let's take a few minutes to explore why Jesus spoke in parables before we begin preparing our dramatic parables.**

Tough Thinking

(10 to 15 minutes)

Form groups of no more than four and have groups each read Matthew 13:10-17. Have kids discuss the following questions in their groups:

■ **Why did Jesus speak in parables?** (To confuse people; so people would have to think about how the message applied to them.)

■ **What's most difficult to understand about this passage?** (Why Jesus would want to confuse people; why some people would understand parables and others wouldn't.)

Have volunteers from each group report their answers. Then say: **Think back to the analogies we made at the beginning of this lesson. In each group, review what occupation you named to describe yourself. Then see if you can determine what each person was really saying about himself or herself by naming that particular occupation. After you've spent about a minute discussing one person, have that person explain what the analogy meant to him or her.**

Allow five minutes or so for groups to discuss their analogies. Then ask the following questions and have groups discuss them before sharing their insights with the whole class:

■ **What did you discover as you explored what you thought the analogies meant?** (We learned about that person's interests; we learned that person had a sense of humor.)

■ **How did you learn more about a person by discussing the analogies than you would have if the person had simply explained his or her interests?** (We asked lots of questions; we learned something more than interests; we learned about the person's personality.)

Say: **Just as we can discover more about a person by exploring a comparison he or she makes, we can discover much about faith by exploring Jesus' parables. This week we'll begin by exploring the parable that surrounds Jesus' explanation of why he speaks in parables. Then we'll brainstorm one or more ways to bring this parable to life with a dramatic parable presentation.**

Parable Beginning

(20 to 25 minutes)

Explain the dramatic-parable concept to kids by using the following description: **During the next four weeks we'll be creating dramatic parables for the whole church to see. A dramatic parable is simply an enactment of the parable's message. We can choose from a variety of ways to create our dramatic parables, including**

■ **frozen statues (people freeze like mannequins into specific positions that depict a scene from the parable),**

■ **loop skits (short skits that repeat over and over again),** and

■ **interactive skits (skits that involve the congregation members in some way).**

You may come up with other ways of expressing Jesus' parables, too.

Form parable groups of no more than six and assign each group Matthew 13:1-9. (This is the only week all groups will work on the same parable.)

Distribute a photocopy of the "Dramatic-Parable Process" handout (p. 16) to each group. Have kids list their Scripture passage at the top of their handout. Lead kids in following the instructions on the handout.

PROJECT WORK

Teacher Tip

If you have a large class, creating parable groups will allow you to split the class into more manageable sizes for planning and implementing the dramatic parables. You may want to have additional adult help for each parable group.

This is the only week all parable groups are required to act out the same parable. In coming weeks they'll be encouraged to choose different parables to act out.

A Step-by-Step Guide for Creating Dramatic Parables

Use the following tips to help groups through each step of the process:

Step 1. Have volunteers read the Bible passage to their parable groups.

Step 2. This is an important step in the process of creating the dramatic parable. Help parable groups explore the parable they've been assigned as if they were there when Jesus first told it. The parable of the sower is explained in detail in Matthew 13:18-23. Encourage kids to look up this passage and discuss it. Also, make Bible commentaries available for those groups that want to study the parable in greater detail.

Step 3. This is an important checkpoint for you. Spend time with each parable group to hear their discoveries about how the parable applies to them today. If their conclusions seem off the mark, help them get back on target by suggesting alternative applications or by redirecting them to the main point of the parable. The more simply kids can define the purpose of the parable, the easier it is to create a dramatic parable.

Step 4. Encourage variety in the ways parable groups dramatize their parables. The parable of the sower, for example, lends itself nicely to a loop skit, where kids silently act out each part over and over while congregation members look on.

Step 5. Remind kids they can use props for their parables, including specific areas of your church building or grounds. For example, if kids choose to perform the parable of the sower outside, the person who represents the sun might stand on a balcony or on a ledge outside the church.

Step 6. Help kids choose the best time to perform their skits. After you determine what each parable group is doing, you can help schedule the skits so they get maximum exposure to the congregation. For example, a loop skit based on the parable of the sower would be a great skit to perform as people arrive to worship. Have kids set up their skit 20 minutes before worship and begin performing it as people arrive. Or have kids perform the skit just after worship and before the Christian education hour. You'll need to adjust times based on your church schedule.

Step 7. Have poster board and markers available for kids to use during this step. Get church members thinking about the dramatic parables by creating questions based on the passage. List them on a poster near the dramatic presentation. For example, next to the parable of the sower, a poster might list the following:

Matthew 13:1-9

■ What does this parable mean to you?

■ What can we do to help others receive God's Word more willingly?

■ How is God using you to sow the seed of God's Word?

By the end of this planning time, parable groups should have a good idea about how they'll act out their parable, what props and posters they'll need, and when they'll meet to perform it.

Preparing the Teaser

(10 to 15 minutes)

The teaser is an important part of this course. During this time kids will determine publicity—how to keep adults and other congregation members informed about the dramatic parable.

Note: Because the dramatic parable idea may be new and unusual to your church, plan on making your own announcement during the next worship service to explain what your class is up to. Tell church members to expect new dramatic parables each week and encourage them to observe, participate, and interact with the students as called for by the dramatic presentation. Then have kids present their teaser for the first dramatic parable.

Your first teaser can be presented today or when the kids actually perform the first dramatic parable.

If your worship service follows your class time, have kids prepare a teaser that can be presented during the service or immediately following the service (with kids stationed in the narthex or outside the church).

If your worship service preceded this class time (or you're meeting during the week), have kids prepare a teaser to present during next week's worship.

Give each parable group a copy of the "Preparing the Teaser" handout (p. 17). Have groups each create their own teaser idea for the first dramatic parable following the instructions on the handout.

When the groups have prepared their teasers, have them each tell what they're planning to do. Then review responsibilities for the teasers and parable presentations before continuing.

Parable Review

(5 to 10 minutes)

Have kids form a large circle for a brief review of today's parable. Ask the following questions one at a time and have kids take turns answering them. Not everyone must answer each question, but encourage each class member to answer at least once. Ask:

■ **What did you enjoy most about working on this project today?**

■ **What did you learn about parables today?**

■ **What was most difficult for you to understand about today's parable?**

■ **How can we use parables today to help others know more about the Christian faith?**

Teacher Tip

Have parable groups each work on a different teaser. Some groups might create posters while others might prepare announcements to present during worship. Work with each group to avoid duplicate teaser ideas.

Teacher Tip

It's possible that some class members will be absent when parable groups present their teasers or the actual dramatic parables. It may be necessary to combine two groups if this happens, so all kids can participate in a dramatic parable. Or, kids might want to choose members of another youth group class (or adults) to fill in on the day they present their teaser or dramatic parable.

Table Talk

The "Table Talk" activity in this course helps young people explore Jesus' parables with their families. If you choose to use the "Table Talk" activity, this is a good time to show students the "Table Talk" handout (p. 18). Ask them to spend time with their parents completing it.

Before kids leave, give them each the "Table Talk" handout to take home or tell them you'll be sending it to their parents. Tell kids to be prepared to report next week on their experiences with the handout. Or use the "Table Talk" idea found in the Bonus Ideas (p. 37) for a meeting based on the handout.

Thanks for Insight
(up to 5 minutes)

Have kids form their parable groups into circles for this closing activity. Beginning with the person who has the most colorful shoes, have that person say one thing he or she appreciated about the person on his or her left during class. For example, someone might say, "I was glad you were in our group because you made great posters" or "I appreciated your good ideas in our group."

Then have parable groups close with a prayer similar to this one: **Thank you, God, for giving us good minds to uncover the spiritual truths in parables, and thank you for the gift of each other. Help us to bring truth to life for others as we present our dramatic parables in the coming weeks.**

Thank students for attending.

If kids will be presenting a teaser during worship immediately following class, determine a place to meet. Let the pastor or "announcement maker" know your class will be presenting an announcement during worship.

Otherwise, remind kids when they need to be at church next week. Having kids come a few minutes early allows them time to practice their teaser or make last-minute preparations for their parable presentations.

If You Still Have Time...

What Luke Wrote—Have kids study Luke 8:4-15 and compare this version of the parable of the sower with that recorded in Matthew 13:1-23.

Parable Rap—Have parable groups develop raps or rhymes describing their parable and what it means for today. Then consider having groups present these rhymes or raps along with their dramatic parables. Or have them present them to other church-school classes.

DRAMATIC-PARABLE PROCESS

Use this handout as a guide for creating your dramatic parables for the coming week.

Scripture passage: _____

Step 1.

Follow along in your Bible while one person reads the parable aloud.

Step 2.

In your parable groups, discuss what the parable meant in Jesus' time. You may need to refer to Bible commentaries for a better understanding of the situation.

Step 3.

In your parable groups, discuss the parable's meaning for today. Answer questions such as "What does this mean for me?" and "How can I apply this message to my own life?"

Step 4.

Brainstorm ways your group could dramatize this parable. See ideas in the box at the bottom of this page.

Step 5.

Determine which method you'll use for creating your dramatic parable, choose your props and location, and practice your dramatic parable.

Step 6.

Choose when you'll do your dramatic parable and for how long. A typical frozen skit or loop skit might last anywhere from 10 to 20 minutes. An interactive skit might last anywhere from five minutes to half an hour and could be performed before, during, or after worship.

Step 7.

Determine what signs, if any, you'll need to set up next to your dramatic parable. You might want to list the Scripture passage or a few questions for observers to think about based on the parable. When you've determined what you'll need, prepare the signs using the available supplies.

Dramatic-Parable Methods

- Frozen statues (kids frozen like mannequins into specific positions that depict a scene from the parable)
- Loop skits (short skits that repeat over and over again)
- Interactive skits (skits that involve the congregation members in some way)

PREPARING THE TEASER

A teaser is an advertisement for your upcoming dramatic parable. It is the publicity that lets adults and other congregation members know what you're up to.

Here are some teaser examples (make up your own ideas, too):

■ posters,

■ announcements during worship,

■ fliers describing what's coming next week,

■ short versions of the skit presented during worship,

■ cryptic clues about the upcoming parable (using words or pictures) scattered around the church,

■ mentions in the church newsletter,

■ clues scattered about the sanctuary, and

■ information listed in the bulletin.

When preparing your teaser, answer the following questions to make sure you don't forget anything:

■ What kind of teaser will you present?

■ What will each group member do for the teaser?

■ What supplies (if any) do you need for your teaser?

■ If your teaser is an announcement, who will let the person who coordinates announcements know you'll need a couple of minutes?

■ If your teaser is a poster, where will you place it?

■ List any other responsibilities for group members below:

Table Talk

To the Parent: We're involved in a youth course at church called *Acting Out Jesus' Parables*. Students are exploring the meaning of Jesus' parables through skits, human sculptures, and other creative experiences.

We'd like you and your teenager to spend some time discussing Jesus' parables. Use this "Table Talk" page to help you do that.

Parent

- What were the most memorable lessons you learned in school or church?
- Which of Jesus' parables do you relate to most? (If you're unfamiliar with Jesus' parables, read the book of Matthew or Luke with your teenager and explore the parables together.)
- Parables use the culture of the time to explain a spiritual truth. What activities, events, and experiences might Jesus refer to if he were to create parables based on your teenage years?

Teenager

- What intrigues you most about the way Jesus taught?
- How do you learn best?
- If Jesus were writing parables based on your world, what activities, events, and experiences might Jesus use as comparisons?

Parent and teenager

- What can we learn from Jesus' parables?
- What's most important to understand about the way Jesus taught his disciples?
- Why is it important to explore the meaning of Jesus' parables?
- Why didn't Jesus simply tell people what was right or wrong?

Together, read the following parables. Then discuss what they might have meant during Jesus' time and what they mean for today:

Luke 10:25-37
Luke 14:16-24
Luke 15:11-32

Extra! Extra!

For fun, create a parable about your family. Tell it like a story, then write it down to keep in a scrapbook for future reference. Design it to reflect truths about your family.

Lifestyle Parables

Many of Jesus' parables focused on lifestyle issues such as wealth, faithfulness, mercy, and humility. As teenagers explore these parables, they'll discover important truths they can apply to their own lifestyles.

Students will explore parables that describe the Christian lifestyle and plan dramatic representations of those parables.

Students will
■ explore Jesus' parables about lifestyle issues,
■ determine what Jesus' parables mean for us today, and
■ create dramatic parables.

Look up the following key Bible passages. Then read the background paragraphs to see how each passage relates to your young people. These Scriptures will be explored during the Bible study portion of today's lesson.

In **Luke 10:25-37**; **14:16-24**; **18:1-14**; and **19:12-27**, Jesus tells parables relating truths about the Christian lifestyle.

The parables in these passages focus on what Christians must be concerned about—issues that affect our daily lives.

In the parable of the good Samaritan (Luke 10:25-37), Jesus teaches not only about our neighbors but that we should show mercy to others. In the parable about the banquet guests (Luke 14:16-24), Jesus reminds us of the danger of indifference in our lives. The parable of the unfair judge (Luke 18:1-8) reminds us to always pray and have hope even when things don't look hopeful. The parable of the Pharisee and the tax collector (Luke 18:9-14) teaches about humility, and the parable of the three servants (Luke 19:12-27) teaches the value of faithfulness.

The messages in these parables can help young people know what it means to be a Christian. By exploring the parables, kids can learn the value of prayer, faithfulness, mercy, and hope. And they can discover the danger of indifference in spiritual matters.

LESSON AIM

OBJECTIVES

BIBLE BASIS

LUKE 10:25-37
LUKE 14:16-24
LUKE 18:1-14
LUKE 19:12-27

Section	Minutes	What Students Will Do	Supplies
Introduction	5 to 10	**Lifestyles**—Learn what today's lesson is about and discuss admirable lifestyles.	
Bible Study	10 to 15	**Lifestyle Choices**—Uncover spiritual truths about lifestyle issues from Jesus' parables.	Snack foods, Bibles
Project Work	20 to 25	**Parable Beginning**—Begin work on their second dramatic parable.	Poster supplies, Bibles, "Dramatic-Parable Process" handouts (p. 16), pencils, Bible commentaries
	10 to 15	**Preparing the Teaser**—Plan advertisements for the upcoming dramatic parables.	Poster supplies, "Preparing the Teaser" handouts (p. 17), pencils
	5 to 10	**Parable Review**—Briefly review the messages in today's parables.	
Closing	5 to 10	**Lifestyle Commitments**—Make commitments to follow Jesus' lifestyle teachings.	

The Lesson

INTRODUCTION

Lifestyles

(5 to 10 minutes)

Welcome students to the class. Say: **In this, our second week exploring Jesus' parables, we're going to examine parables that help us know more about the Christian lifestyle. And we're going to plan ways to live out these parables for the whole congregation to enjoy.**

Open with prayer. As a review, have a volunteer tell a definition of a parable. If necessary repeat the following definition from the first lesson: **A parable is a figure of speech in which a spiritual truth (or moral) is illustrated by something drawn from everyday experience.**

Say: **Since today's parables focus on lifestyle issues, let's begin by telling each other whose lifestyle we admire. Later we'll compare how these lifestyles match up to the spiritual truths in Jesus' parables.**

Form groups of no more than four and have kids each tell whose lifestyle they admire. Kids might choose famous people, relatives, or friends. Then have kids tell why they admire those people's lifestyles.

After a couple of minutes, call kids together and have volunteers explain what they admire about the person they chose. Ask:

■ **What are lifestyle traits people often strive to attain?**
(Wealth; happiness; truth.)

■ **How does our relationship with God shape our lifestyle?**
(We make different decisions because we love God; we don't care as much about worldly things.)

Say: **Jesus has a lot to say about the way we live. Today we'll learn what Jesus teaches about the Christian lifestyle through his parables.**

Lifestyle Choices

(10 to 15 minutes)

Bring out a plate of doughnuts or other treats. Say: **If you want these doughnuts, ask me for them.**

When kids ask for the food, don't let them have it. Continue to say "no" until kids begin to get frustrated. After a minute or two, ask:

■ **How does it feel to ask for this snack and not be allowed to have it?** (Frustrating; it seems hopeless.)

Say: **In one of Jesus' parables on lifestyle issues, an unfair judge refuses to hear a woman's rightful complaint. But because of her persistence and his own aggravation at her continued request, the judge finally gives in and grants the woman her rights.**

Don't say any more. Kids will probably ask again for the doughnuts. If they do, give them out happily. If they don't, remind kids again of the message in Jesus' parable and tell them they must remain hopeful and persistent (and ask for the doughnuts again).

Ask:

■ **What do this activity and Jesus' parable tell us about hope and prayer?** (We must be persistent; don't give up; pray all the time.)

Say: **Jesus taught many things in his lifestyle parables. We'll explore just a few of them today.**

Form up to five groups of at least four people each. Assign each group one of the following Scripture passages: **Luke 10:25-37; Luke 14:16-24; Luke 18:1-8; Luke 18:9-14; Luke 19:12-27.**

If you have fewer than five groups, assign more than one passage to each group.

Say: **Take the next five minutes to read your passage and determine the central issue of the parable.** If kids have trouble uncovering an issue, refer to the Bible Basis on page 19. Use that information to help students discover the parable's theme.

After groups have read and briefly discussed their parables, have someone in each group share his or her group's conclusions with the whole class.

Then ask the following questions, allowing time for groups to discuss them before having volunteers tell the whole group what they discussed. Ask:

■ **What do these parables teach about the Christian lifestyle?** (We should pray often; we need to be humble; don't be indifferent to spiritual things.)

■ **How do the people whose lifestyles we admire measure up to the messages of these parables?** (Answers will vary.)

■ **What can we do to better follow Jesus' teachings in these parables?** (Pray daily; trust God when things are bad; spend time thinking about spiritual matters; be humble.)

Say: **Now that we have a basic understanding of these parables, let's begin work on our dramatic parables. Remember to focus your dramatic-parable presentations on the *meaning* of the parable—not just the action that takes place.**

PROJECT WORK

Parable Beginning

(20 to 25 minutes)

As a quick review (and to help new attendees and visitors understand the format for this course), repeat this explanation of the dramatic-parable concept: **Once again we're going to explore Jesus' parables and create dramatic parables based on what we learn. A dramatic parable is simply an enactment of the parable's message.**

Give kids each a new copy of the "Dramatic-Parable Process" handout (p. 16). Then form parable groups of no more than six. Today you have five parables to choose from for your parable groups. You may assign a different parable to each group or assign the same parable to more than one group.

The parables are
■ Luke 10:25-37 (the good Samaritan),
■ Luke 14:16-24 (the banquet guests),
■ Luke 18:1-8 (the unfair judge),
■ Luke 18:9-14 (the Pharisee and the tax collector), and
■ Luke 19:12-27 (the three servants).

As you assign the parables, lead parable groups in following the handout instructions.

Refer to "A Step-by-Step Guide for Creating Dramatic Parables" on page 13 from lesson 1, "Planning the Project." Use the ideas in the "Idea Sparks" box below to get kids thinking about how to enact this week's parables.

Teacher Tip

If you have a large class, creating parable groups will allow you to split the class into more manageable sizes for planning and implementing the dramatic parables. You may want to have additional adult help for each parable group.

Idea Sparks

Here are a few starter ideas to spark kids' creativity for this week's dramatic-parable presentations.

Parable of the Good Samaritan (Luke 10:25-37)

■ Invite adult participation in this interactive skit by having them help the man who was beaten and robbed.

■ Arrange ahead of time to have your pastor, or another prominent person in your church, play the part of the person who is beaten and robbed (or other key roles).

■ If you prepare a poster for the parable, consider listing the following questions:

Who in this skit are you most like?

Who is your neighbor?

How can you show mercy to your neighbors?

(continued on next page)

Parable of the Banquet Guests (Luke 14:16-24)

■ Perform this skit in the middle of a church service, inviting congregation members to play the parts of the banquet guests.

■ Change the setting to modern times and have one person "call" a bunch of friends inviting them to a party.

■ If you prepare a poster for the parable, consider listing the following questions:

What kind of banquet guest would you be?

What are the dangers of indifference in our faith?

Parable of the Unfair Judge (Luke 18:1-8)

■ Perform this as a "loop" skit and have nonacting kids form a chorus to tell the story through short rhymes.

■ Perform this during worship. Let your pastor know your kids will pester him or her to illustrate the theme of persistence and hope. Have kids come up to the front of the church, pray, and then ask the pastor for something (such as a moment to talk with the congregation).

■ If you prepare a poster for the parable, consider listing the following questions:

Why do people give up on things they hope for?

What does this parable tell us about prayer and hope?

Parable of the Pharisee and the Tax Collector (Luke 18:9-14)

■ This parable works well as a loop skit performed outside on the steps of the church. The louder the Pharisee character, the better!

■ Or, have kids perform this during a regular offering time (with the pastor's knowledge, of course). The kids or the pastor could then debrief the skit with the congregation.

■ If you prepare a poster for the parable, consider listing the following questions:

In what areas of your life are you more like the Pharisee? the tax collector?

What is the role of humility in Christian faith?

How can we be more humble in our faith lives?

Parable of the Three Servants (Luke 19:12-27)

■ Have kids perform this skit before or after worship and use congregation members as the money in the story. The servants would then collect more people (money) to represent the fruits of their investments.

■ Have kids modernize this story. For example, a wealthy businessperson who owns three music stores must leave the country, so he or she places the stores in the hands of three managers.

■ If you prepare a poster for the parable, consider listing the following questions:

How are you investing your faith?

What is the role of faithfulness in your life?

How can we be more like the servants who invested the money?

Preparing the Teaser

(10 to 15 minutes)

Give parable groups each a new copy of the "Preparing the Teaser" handout (p. 17). Have parable groups each create their

Teacher Tip

It's possible that some class members will be absent when parable groups present their teasers or the actual dramatic parables. It may be necessary to combine two groups if this happens so all kids can participate in a dramatic parable. Or, kids might want to choose members of another youth group class (or adults) to fill in on the day they present their teaser or dramatic parable.

CLOSING

own teaser idea for the dramatic parables, following the instructions on the handout.

When the groups have prepared their teasers, have them each share with the class what they're planning to do. Then review responsibilities for the teasers and dramatic parables before continuing.

Parable Review
(5 to 10 minutes)

Have kids form a large circle for a brief review of today's parable. Ask the following questions one at a time and have kids take turns answering them. Not everyone must answer each question, but encourage each class member to answer at least once. Ask:

■ **What did you enjoy most about working on this project today?**

■ **What was most difficult for you to understand about today's parables?**

■ **How can we use parables today to help others know more about faith?**

Lifestyle Commitments
(5 to 10 minutes)

Form a circle. Have kids each complete the following sentence, filling in one lifestyle choice they'll commit to based on today's parables: **With God's help, I commit to...** For example, someone might say, "I commit to being hopeful and praying often" or "I commit to being more humble."

Close by having kids practice the message of Jesus' parable of the unfair judge—have kids spend one or two minutes in silent prayer.

Thank kids for attending.

If kids will be presenting a teaser during worship immediately following class, determine a place to meet and be sure to let the pastor or "announcement maker" know you'll be presenting an announcement during worship.

Otherwise, remind kids when they need to be at church next week. Having kids come a few minutes early allows them time to practice their teaser or make last-minute preparations for their dramatic parables.

If You Still Have Time...

Other Lifestyle Choices—Have kids explore Paul's lifestyle teachings in Ephesians 4:17-32. Form groups of no more than four to explore these teachings and compare them with Jesus' parables. Have kids determine how these lifestyle teachings apply to them.

Kingdom Parables

PART ONE

Many Christians have a difficult time understanding what God's kingdom is all about. Some equate God's kingdom with heaven. Others know it has something to do with Christians today but aren't quite sure how it relates to them.

Jesus used parables to shed light on many aspects of God's kingdom. In this, the first of two lessons on the subject, young people will piece together glimpses of God's kingdom and how it applies to them today. Next week they'll explore the future aspects of God's kingdom.

Students will explore parables about God's kingdom and plan dramatic representations of those parables.

LESSON AIM

Students will
- explore the meaning of Jesus' parables,
- determine how Jesus' parables apply to their lives, and
- create dramatic parables.

OBJECTIVES

Look up the following key Bible passages. Then read the background paragraphs to see how each passage relates to your young people. These Scriptures will be explored during the Bible study portion of today's lesson.

BIBLE BASIS

MATTHEW 13:31-46
MATTHEW 20:1-16

In **Matthew 13:31-46 and 20:1-16,** Jesus uses parables to describe God's kingdom.

In these passages, Jesus uses parables to shed light on what it means to be a part of God's kingdom. In Matthew 20:1-16, the parable of the vineyard workers, Jesus teaches how people will be received into God's kingdom. It illustrates the importance of seizing the opportunities we've been given, not our length of service.

In the parables of the mustard seed and the yeast (Matthew 13:31-33), Jesus relates the importance of spreading the gospel to the world. These short parables illustrate that the kingdom of God is relevant for the present as well as the future.

In the parables of the treasure and the pearl (Matthew 13:44-46), Jesus describes the immeasurable value of choosing to follow Christ.

What is Jesus' message in these kingdom parables? Do all that you can to build the kingdom of God today. Or, in simpler terms, share Christ's love with everyone *now* because a time is coming when Christians will be separated from non-Christians.

Teenagers may understand the future aspects of God's kingdom—eternal life with God. But they can discover from Jesus' parables that God's kingdom begins now. And they can learn the importance of living in God's kingdom and sharing God's love with others.

THIS LESSON AT A GLANCE

Section	Minutes	What Students Will Do	Supplies
Introduction	5 to 10	**God's Kingdom**—Discuss the plan for today's lesson and explore why people choose to be Christians.	
Bible Study	10 to 15	**The Now and the Not Yet**—Discover the dual nature of God's kingdom and study parables in Matthew 13:31-46 and 20:1-16.	Bibles, paper, pencils, snacks
Project Work	20 to 25	**Parable Beginning**—Begin work on their third dramatic parable.	Poster supplies, Bibles, "Dramatic-Parable Process" handouts (p. 16), pencils, Bible commentaries
	10 to 15	**Preparing the Teaser**—Plan advertisements for the upcoming dramatic parables.	Poster supplies, "Preparing the Teaser" handouts (p. 17), pencils
	5 to 10	**Parable Review**—Briefly review the messages in today's parables.	
Closing	5 to 10	**In the Kingdom**—Affirm each other's kingdom traits.	Paper crowns

The Lesson

God's Kingdom

(5 to 10 minutes)

INTRODUCTION

Welcome students to the class. Say: **In this, our third week of exploring Jesus' parables, we're going to examine parables that help us know more about God's kingdom, and plan ways to live out these parables for the whole congregation to enjoy.**

Open with prayer. As a review, have a volunteer tell the definition of a parable.

Say: **Some of Jesus' parables about God's kingdom help us understand what it means to be a Christian. Let's begin today's lesson by calling out why people are Christians.**

Have kids call out reasons people become Christians. Kids might say things such as "because their family is Christian," "because they love God" or "because they want to go to heaven."

Say: **People become Christians for different reasons. And one common reason people believe in Christ is because they want to go to heaven. While no one can fault anyone for choosing heaven over hell, Jesus teaches that the kingdom of God is more than in our future—it's something Christians participate in now. We're going to explore some of Jesus' parables about how Christians live in God's kingdom today.**

The Now and the Not Yet
(10 to 15 minutes)

Tell kids you have an important message for them. Have kids huddle around you, then say: **Listen carefully during today's lesson because at the end of the Bible study activity...** Don't finish your sentence. Kids may wonder what you're up to, but don't give in and tell them. Simply move on to the next part of the Bible study.

Form groups of no more than four. Say: **In your group choose who'll be the reader (who reads the Bible passage), who'll be the leader (who'll lead the group's discussion about the passages), who'll be the note-taker (who'll list the group's discoveries about the parables), and who'll be the reporter (who'll share those discoveries with the whole class).**

Give each note-taker a sheet of paper and a pencil. Have groups read Matthew 13:31-46 and 20:1-16 and discuss what the parables say about God's kingdom. Allow five to seven minutes for groups to discuss the passages, then call time and have reporters share their group's discoveries. Ask:

■ **Based on your studies, what's important to understand about God's kingdom?** (God's kingdom is happening now; God's kingdom is something valuable.)

■ **How did you feel when I told you to listen carefully but didn't fully explain why?** (Confused; I thought you were planning a surprise.)

Give kids a snack and explain that this is what you hinted about at the beginning of the Bible Study. Ask:

■ **How is the way I told you to listen carefully, but didn't tell everything about what was coming, like the way Jesus uses parables to explain what it's like to be in God's kingdom?** (Jesus taught us how to act now; Jesus taught about the coming kingdom, just as you told us something was coming, too.)

Say: **God's kingdom is something we participate in as Christians. Just as I gave you instructions for now (to listen carefully) and promised something to come (the snack), Jesus taught his disciples how to live in the kingdom today and promised something wonderful for the future. And just as you didn't know what was coming in the future, we won't fully understand what God has planned for us in heaven until we get there.**

Allow kids to enjoy their snacks as they begin working on their dramatic parables.

Teacher Tip

If you have a large class, creating parable groups will allow you to split the class into more manageable sizes for planning and implementing the dramatic parables. You may want to have additional adult help for each parable group.

Parable Beginning

(20 to 25 minutes)

As a quick review (and to help new attendees and visitors understand the format for this course), repeat this explanation of the dramatic-parable concept: **Once again we're going to explore Jesus' parables and create dramatic parables based on what we learn. A dramatic parable is simply an enactment of the parable's message.**

Give kids each a new copy of the "Dramatic-Parable Process" handout (p. 16). Then form parable groups of no more than six. Today you have five short parables to choose from for your parable groups. You may assign a different parable to each group or assign the same parable to more than one group.

The parables are
- Matthew 13:31-32 (the mustard seed),
- Matthew 13:33 (the yeast),
- Matthew 13:44 (the treasure),
- Matthew 13:45-46 (the pearl), and
- Matthew 20:1-16 (the vineyard workers).

As you assign the parables, lead parable groups in following the handout instructions.

Refer to "A Step-by-Step Guide for Creating Dramatic Parables" on page 13 from lesson 1, "Planning the Project." Use the ideas in the "Idea Sparks" box below to get kids thinking about how to enact this week's parables.

Idea Sparks

Here are a few starter ideas to spark kids' creativity for this week's dramatic parable presentations.

Parable of the Mustard Seed and Parable of the Yeast (Matthew 13:31-33)
- Kids might illustrate the mustard seed's immense growth by unrolling crepe paper and handing it to church members during a worship service.
- Kids could actually bake bread as a part of their skit and compare unleavened bread to bread that has risen because of yeast.
- Teenagers might act out the growth of the mustard tree by starting out all bunched together and then branching out among the church. (This would make a great loop skit.)

Parable of the Treasure and Parable of the Pearl (Matthew 13:44-46)
- Kids might go around and ask congregation members to give up something they're carrying.
- Kids could hide a treasure in the church sanctuary, then find it during the church service and attempt to "trade" with the people seated there for the pew or chairs near the treasure.
- If you prepare a poster for the parable, consider writing something like the following on the poster: "Matthew 13:45-46. Read it. Then decide...what would you sell for the pearl? What do you need to give up for Christ?"

(continued on next page)

Parable of the Vineyard Workers (Matthew 20:1-16)

■ Teenagers might give each person who enters the church a fake dollar for "doing God's work." Then some of the teenagers could come in late and act the part of the disgruntled vineyard workers.

■ A frozen statue illustrating the parable of the vineyard workers could be set up just outside the sanctuary before or after a worship service.

■ Kids might modernize this parable to focus on the concept of being willing to serve no matter when you come to serve. Kids could change the setting to be a fund-raiser, where some kids come late but do their share of work and get the same pizza reward.

Preparing the Teaser
(10 to 15 minutes)

Give parable groups each a new copy of the "Preparing the Teaser" handout (p. 17). Have parable groups each create their own teaser idea for the dramatic parables, following the instructions on the handout.

When the groups have prepared their teasers, have them each share with the class what they're planning to do. Then review responsibilities for the teasers and dramatic parables before continuing.

Parable Review
(5 to 10 minutes)

Have kids form pairs for a brief review of today's parable. Ask the following questions one at a time and have partners take turns answering them. Then have volunteers share their partners' answers with the whole group. Ask:

■ **What did you enjoy most about working on this project today?**

■ **What was most difficult for you to understand about today's parables?**

■ **How can we use parables to help others know more about God's kingdom?**

■ **How are Christians members of God's kingdom today?**

In the Kingdom
(5 to 10 minutes)

Form a circle. Give each person a marker and a paper crown (see illustration in the margin for one way to create the crowns).

Say: As you've worked together on these dramatic parables, you've probably discovered some positive traits in each other. Let's use these paper crowns to say thanks to each other and say what positive "kingdom traits" we see in each other.

CLOSING

Have kids take turns standing in the center of the circle, holding their paper crowns. Have other class members walk up to the person in the center and silently write a positive trait on that person's crown. For example, someone might write "You're a great listener" or "You've been a good friend."

Remind kids to write only positive traits and to be sincere. To ensure each person is affirmed, you may choose to call on people to write on others' crowns. Or add your own affirmations to each person's crown.

Have kids each wear their crown as you close in prayer.

If kids will be presenting a teaser during worship immediately following class, determine a place to meet and be sure to let the pastor or "announcement maker" know you'll be presenting an announcement during worship.

Otherwise, remind kids when they need to be at church next week. Having kids come a few minutes early allows them time to practice their teaser or make last-minute preparations for their dramatic parables.

Thank students for attending.

If You Still Have Time . . .

The Kingdom Life—Form groups of no more than four and have kids discuss what it means to them to be in God's kingdom today. Have students focus on what it takes to be a member of God's kingdom in everyday situations at school, home, work, and church.

Kingdom Song—Have kids write a song (using a familiar tune) that describes what it means to be a member of God's kingdom today. Encourage kids to refer to the parables they studied today for ideas to include in their song.

Kingdom Parables

PART TWO

Jesus' kingdom parables teach us not only how to live in God's kingdom today, but how people will be chosen to live in God's future kingdom—heaven. In these parables Jesus' message is one of urgency. Since Christ could return at any time, we must do all we can to share the gospel now.

In this second lesson on Jesus' kingdom parables, young people will discover Jesus' concern for urgency and determine how they can share the good news with others.

Students will explore parables about God's kingdom and plan dramatic representations of those parables.

Students will
- explore the meaning of Jesus' parables,
- determine how Jesus' parables apply to their lives, and
- create dramatic parables.

Look up the following key Bible passages. Then read the background paragraphs to see how each passage relates to your teenagers. These Scriptures will be explored during the Bible study portion of today's lesson.

In **Matthew 13:24-30; 13:47-50; and 25:1-13**, Jesus uses parables to teach about the coming kingdom of God.

In these three parables Jesus focuses his message on the future aspects of God's kingdom.

In the parable of the wheat and weeds (Matthew 13:24-30), Jesus explains why there is evil in the world and what will become of those who are evil at the end of the world. This passage is significant for Christians today because it reminds us that God's people constantly battle "weeds" as we move toward the end of the world. While there is certainly a future aspect to this parable, the immediate message is one of endurance and patience for those who love God.

In the parable of the fishing net (Matthew 13:47-50), Jesus describes how the angels will separate the good people from the bad and describes what's in store for those who are in the bad category.

The parable of the 10 bridesmaids (Matthew 25:1-13) raises the

LESSON AIM

OBJECTIVES

BIBLE BASIS

MATTHEW 13:24-30

MATTHEW 13:47-50

MATTHEW 25:1-13

stakes as Jesus teaches about the importance of being prepared for Christ's return. This parable portrays a sense of urgency in our role as evangelists—people who share God's love with others.

Each of these three parables gives us a glimpse of God's just nature. At the same time they remind us that God is so much greater than our understanding. By helping young people understand these parables, we can motivate them to reach out with God's love to others.

THIS LESSON AT A GLANCE

Section	Minutes	What Students Will Do	Supplies
Introduction	5 to 10	**Heavenly Thoughts**—Share ideas of what heaven will be like.	Bubbles, confetti, streamers
Bible Study	10 to 15	**Urgency**—Learn about the urgency of sharing the gospel and explore Jesus' parables about the coming kingdom of God.	Pennies, cup, Bibles
Project Work	20 to 25	**Parable Beginning**—Learn the process for creating dramatic parables and begin work on their dramatic parables.	Poster supplies, Bibles "Dramatic-Parable Process" handouts (p. 16), pencils, Bible commentaries
	10 to 15	**Preparing the Teaser**—Plan advertisements for the upcoming dramatic parables.	Poster supplies, "Preparing the Teaser" handouts (p. 17), pencils
	5 to 10	**Parable Review**—Briefly review the messages in today's parables.	
Closing	5 to 10	**Tell the World**—Brainstorm ways they'll tell friends about Jesus.	

INTRODUCTION

The Lesson

Heavenly Thoughts

(5 to 10 minutes)

Welcome students to the class. Say: **We've come to the final lesson on living Jesus' parables. Today we'll explore new parables about God's kingdom. And we'll plan how to act these out for the congregation by creating our final dramatic parables.**

Open with a circle prayer. Have students join hands and add a sentence of praise, thanksgiving, or special concerns.

Place bubble-blowing supplies, streamers, and piles of confetti on a table. Then form groups of three. Have kids determine which person in each group is the "bubble," the "streamer," and the "confetti." Then have kids each collect the item that represents them.

Say: **In your group discuss what you think heaven will be like. Make sure each person gets a chance to talk. After each person has spoken, toss the confetti and streamers and blow bubbles to celebrate God's future kingdom.**

After the celebration, have volunteers tell what their trio members thought heaven might be like. Ask:

■ **What was it like to celebrate with your confetti, streamers, and bubbles?** (It was fun; I was embarrassed; it was cool.)

■ **How is that like the way you feel knowing that God has great plans in store for us in heaven?** (Great; comforting; exciting.)

Say: **Last week we explored parables that helped us see how we're a part of God's kingdom now. But today's parables teach us a little about the "not yet," the future kingdom of God. Let's explore those parables briefly before working on our dramatic parables.**

Leave the confetti and streamers on the floor until the closing.

Urgency
(10 to 15 minutes)

Go around the room and drop at least 50 pennies on the floor. Make sure the pennies are spread out around the whole room. If you have more than 20 people in your class, drop at least 75 pennies.

Don't tell kids why you're dropping the pennies. When all the pennies are scattered around the room, hold up a cup and say: **You have an unknown amount of time to collect all the pennies in this room and put them in this cup. Each person may bring only one penny at a time to the cup. Ready... go!**

Before kids finish getting all the pennies to the cup, call time. Have kids collect the rest of the pennies and place them on a table next to the cup. Ask:

■ **How did you feel not knowing how much time you had to collect these pennies?** (Energized; unsure; worried; challenged.)

Say: **Imagine that this cup is heaven and each penny represents a friend. Those pennies that made it into the cup represent people who believed in Jesus. And those pennies that weren't collected represent people who were never told about Christ.** Ask:

■ **How would you feel about those who didn't make it to heaven?** (Sad; I couldn't do anything about it; we tried the best we could.)

■ **How is this activity like or unlike the way people will make it into heaven?** (We don't know when Christ will return; not everyone will get into heaven; this was random, but in real life each person has a choice.)

Say: **Jesus' parables about God's kingdom remind us that Christ could return any time. Let's look at three of these parables and what they mean for us today.**

Form three groups. A group can be two people. Assign each group one of the following Scripture passages:
- Matthew 13:24-30 (the wheat and weeds),
- Matthew 13:47-50 (the fishing net), and
- Matthew 25:1-13 (the 10 bridesmaids).

Say: **Take the next five minutes to read your passage and determine the parable's central issue.** If kids have trouble uncovering an issue, refer to the Bible Basis on page 31 and use that information to help kids discover the parable's theme.

After groups have read and briefly discussed their parables, have someone in each group share their group's conclusions with the whole class.

Then ask the following questions, allowing time for groups to discuss them before having volunteers tell the whole class what they discussed. Ask:

■ **What do these parables teach about the coming kingdom of God?** (The good will be separated from the bad; be prepared; some people will be saved.)

■ **How do these parables apply to us?** (We should follow God; we should tell others about Christ; we must always be ready for Christ's return.)

■ **What are ways we can live out the messages of these parables in everyday life?** (Tell friends about Christ; pray for those who don't know Jesus; be a good example for others to see.)

Say: **Now that we've discovered the importance of sharing Christ with others, let's begin work on our dramatic parables. Remember to focus your dramatic-parable presentations on the *meaning* of the parable—not just the action that takes place.**

Parable Beginning
(20 to 25 minutes)

Give kids each a new copy of the "Dramatic-Parable Process" handout (p. 16). Then form parable groups of no more than six. You have three parables to choose from for your parable groups. You may assign a different parable to each group or assign the same parable to more than one group. After assigning the parables, lead groups in following the instructions on the handout.

The parables are
- Matthew 13:24-30 (the wheat and weeds),
- Matthew 13:47-50 (the fishing net), and
- Matthew 25:1-13 (the 10 bridesmaids).

Refer to "A Step-by-Step Guide for Creating Dramatic Parables" on page 13 from lesson 1, "Planning the Project." Use the ideas in the "Idea Sparks" box on page 35 to get kids thinking about how to enact this week's parables.

PROJECT WORK

Teacher Tip

While this is the last scheduled lesson for this course, your students may need to meet together again depending on when they've been acting out their dramatic parables. If kids will be presenting their dramatic parables on a day other than today, plan on spending a few minutes debriefing the course experience after that time. Use the questions for course review found in the "If You Still Have Time..." section (p. 36).

Idea Sparks

Here are a few starter ideas to spark kids' creativity for this week's dramatic parable presentations.

Parable of the Wheat and Weeds (Matthew 13:24-30)

■ This parable might make an interesting frozen statue. Kids could create signs designating who represents the wheat and who represents the weeds.

■ Teenagers could make this interesting by dressing as weeds and placing themselves among the congregation to introduce the theme.

■ If you create a poster for this parable, consider placing the following words on it: "Tell as many weeds as possible about Jesus…the harvest is coming."

Parable of the Fishing Net (Matthew 13:47-50)

■ A volleyball net would make a great fishing net for this parable.

■ Teenagers could perform this skit by sitting around the church, sorting through plastic or paper fish and calling them good or bad fish.

■ As people arrive at a worship service, kids could send them randomly to one side or the other of the sanctuary to sit. Then, during the service, they could act out the skit as if one side of the congregation represented the good fish and the other the bad fish. After making their point kids might tell congregation members they could return to their usual seats.

Parable of the 10 Bridesmaids (Matthew 25:1-13)

■ An interactive skit based on the 10 bridesmaids parable could introduce the worship service. Kids could involve members of the congregation by trying to get them into their seats before a specific time (or before closing the doors to the sanctuary).

■ This parable would also work as a loop skit just outside the church doors. Kids might perform the skit many times as people are arriving.

■ Flashlights make great "lamps," and batteries could represent "oil" in this skit.

■ Perform this skit in a darkened sanctuary for added dramatic effect.

Preparing the Teaser

(10 to 15 minutes)

Give parable groups each a new copy of the "Preparing the Teaser" handout (p. 17). Have parable groups each create their own teaser idea for the dramatic parables, following the instructions on the handout.

When the groups have prepared their teasers, have them each share with the class what they're planning to do. Then review responsibilities for the teasers and dramatic parables before continuing.

Teacher Tip

If you have a large class, creating parable groups will allow you to split the class into more manageable sizes for planning and implementing the dramatic parables. You may want to have additional adult help for each parable group.

Parable Review

(5 to 10 minutes)

Have kids form a large circle for a brief review of today's parables. Ask the following questions one at a time and have kids take turns answering them. Not everyone must answer each question, but encourage each class member to answer at least once. Ask:

■ **What did you enjoy most about working on this project today?**

■ **What was most difficult for you to understand about today's parables?**

■ **How can we follow the messages of Jesus' kingdom parables in our everyday lives?**

CLOSING

Tell the World

(5 to 10 minutes)

Form groups of no more than four. Have groups brainstorm specific ways they can tell friends about Christ. For example, someone might say, "I can invite friends to church" or "I can offer to help a friend who's going through a tough time." Then form a large circle and have kids tell what their group came up with.

Say: **Let's close the lesson by turning to the person on your left and thanking that person for specific things you've appreciated about him or her during the past four weeks. For example, someone might tell another person, "I really enjoyed your ideas for the dramatic parable we did" or "I'm glad I got to know you better in this class."** As kids give their affirmations, have them toss confetti and streamers left over from the "Heavenly Thoughts" activity onto each other to celebrate the positive actions.

If kids will be presenting a teaser during worship immediately following class, determine a place to meet and be sure to let the pastor or "announcement maker" know you'll be presenting an announcement during worship.

Otherwise, remind kids when they need to be at church next. Having kids come a few minutes early allows them time to practice their teaser or make last-minute preparations for their dramatic parables.

If You Still Have Time...

Course Review—Use the following questions to help kids debrief the past four weeks of living out Jesus' parables.

■ What did you learn about Jesus' parables during this course?

■ What did you like most about this course?

■ How will your life be different because of this course?

■ What surprised you most about this course?

Bonus Ideas

Bonus Scriptures—The lessons focus on a select few Scripture passages, but if you'd like to incorporate more Bible readings into a lesson, here are some suggestions:

Isaiah 6:9-10 (God tells the people they will listen but not understand.)

Matthew 18:23-35 (Parable of the unmerciful servant.)

Matthew 22:1-14 (Marriage of the king's son.)

Matthew 25:14-30 (Parable of the talents.)

Mark 4:26-29 (Parable of the secretly growing seed.)

Luke 16:19-31 (The rich man and Lazarus.)

Mall Parables—Have parable groups develop a dramatic parable they can perform at a local shopping center, mall, or other public location. Help kids get permission to perform their skits. Then help coordinate the times for students to act out their skits. If allowed, have pamphlets available inviting passers-by to your church.

Parable Partners—Form parable partners by linking up two teenagers who work well together. Have partners meet weekly to read and discuss Jesus' parables. Provide church resources such as Bible dictionaries, commentaries, and study Bibles for partners to check out while studying the parables. Then meet once a month for partners to share what they've discovered over the past few weeks.

Video Parables—Get someone to videotape the dramatic parables for later viewing. Then meet with kids after the course is finished and have a parable-review time where kids get to view and discuss the videos.

Pass along particularly good videos to adult classes in your church to use as discussion starters when they study the parables.

Parable Service—Help teenagers prepare a worship service for the whole church based on the dramatic parables they've created. During the service kids could act out their dramatic parables, then briefly explain them. Or kids could involve congregation members in the dramatic parables, then invite discussion on what the parables mean for today.

Modern Parables—Form parable construction teams of no more than four and have them create modern parables on spiritual topics they're interested in. Encourage kids to use

MEETINGS AND MORE

PARTY PLEASER

RETREAT IDEA

modern settings for the parables and incorporate the Scripture message.

Make this a fun contest and award prizes for teams with the most creative parables.

Parable Party—Plan a big party following the last week of this course. Invite parents and other adults in the church to provide lots of food for the event. Then have kids choose their favorite games to play. For example, have kids form teams and act out parables for other teams to guess in a parable variation of charades.

During the party have kids recall their favorite experiences while working on the dramatic parables. Review Matthew 13:1-23 (the first lesson's Bible Basis) during the party.

Close the party by having kids each tell which is their favorite parable and why.

Parable-Adventure Retreat—Prepare a retreat adventure for kids where they can explore Jesus' parables. Before the kids arrive, hide parable adventure kits around the retreat site. A parable-adventure kit could consist of a Bible, a Scripture reference for one of Jesus' parables, and instructions on how to study the parable. Some ideas for instructions include
- act out the parable,
- collect items in nature that represent the parable,
- draw a picture of what the parable means to you,
- create an interpretive dance to reflect the parable,
- tell about a time when you felt like a person in this parable,
- explain this parable without using words, and
- create a modern version of this parable.

Throughout the retreat have kids search for the parable-adventure kits and follow the instructions. Have fun with kids as they explore Jesus' parables in unique ways.

CURRICULUM REORDER—TOP PRIORITY

Order now to prepare for your upcoming Sunday school classes, youth ministry meetings, and weekend retreats! Each book includes all teacher and student materials—plus photocopiable handouts—for any size class!

FOR JUNIOR HIGH/MIDDLE SCHOOL:

Accepting Others: Beyond Barriers & Stereotypes
ISBN 1-55945-126-2

Advice to Young Christians: Exploring Paul's Letters
ISBN 1-55945-146-7

Applying the Bible to Life, ISBN 1-55945-116-5

Becoming Responsible, ISBN 1-55945-109-2

Bible Heroes: Joseph, Esther, Mary & Peter
ISBN 1-55945-137-8

Boosting Self-Esteem, ISBN 1-55945-100-9

Building Better Friendships, ISBN 1-55945-138-6

Can Christians Have Fun?, ISBN 1-55945-134-3

Caring for God's Creation, ISBN 1-55945-121-1

Christmas: A Fresh Look, ISBN 1-55945-124-6

Competition, ISBN 1-55945-133-5

Dealing With Death, ISBN 1-55945-112-2

Dealing With Disappointment, ISBN 1-55945-139-4

Doing Your Best, ISBN 1-55945-142-4

Drugs & Drinking, ISBN 1-55945-118-1

Evil and the Occult, ISBN 1-55945-102-5

Genesis: The Beginnings, ISBN 1-55945-111-4

Guys & Girls: Understanding Each Other
ISBN 1-55945-110-6

Handling Conflict, ISBN 1-55945-125-4

Heaven & Hell, ISBN 1-55945-131-9

Is God Unfair?, ISBN 1-55945-108-4

Love or Infatuation?, ISBN 1-55945-128-9

Making Parents Proud, ISBN 1-55945-107-6

Making the Most of School, ISBN 1-55945-113-0

Materialism, ISBN 1-55945-130-0

The Miracle of Easter, ISBN 1-55945-143-2

Miracles!, ISBN 1-55945-117-3

Peace & War, ISBN 1-55945-123-8

Peer Pressure, ISBN 1-55945-103-3

Prayer, ISBN 1-55945-104-1

Reaching Out to a Hurting World, ISBN 1-55945-140-8

Sermon on the Mount, ISBN 1-55945-129-7

Suicide: The Silent Epidemic, ISBN 1-55945-145-9

Telling Your Friends About Christ, ISBN 1-55945-114-9

The Ten Commandments, ISBN 1-55945-127-0

Today's Faith Heroes, ISBN 1-55945-141-6

Today's Media: Choosing Wisely, ISBN 1-55945-144-0

Today's Music: Good or Bad?, ISBN 1-55945-101-7

What Is God's Purpose for Me?, ISBN 1-55945-132-7

What's a Christian?, ISBN 1-55945-105-X

FOR SENIOR HIGH:

1 & 2 Corinthians: Christian Discipleship
ISBN 1-55945-230-7

Angels, Demons, Miracles & Prayer, ISBN 1-55945-235-8

Changing the World, ISBN 1-55945-236-6

Christians in a Non-Christian World
ISBN 1-55945-224-2

Christlike Leadership, ISBN 1-55945-231-5

Communicating With Friends, ISBN 1-55945-228-5

Counterfeit Religions, ISBN 1-55945-207-2

Dating Decisions, ISBN 1-55945-215-3

Dealing With Life's Pressures, ISBN 1-55945-232-3

Deciphering Jesus' Parables, ISBN 1-55945-237-4

Exodus: Following God, ISBN 1-55945-226-9

Exploring Ethical Issues, ISBN 1-55945-225-0

Faith for Tough Times, ISBN 1-55945-216-1

Forgiveness, ISBN 1-55945-223-4

Getting Along With Parents, ISBN 1-55945-202-1

Getting Along With Your Family, ISBN 1-55945-233-1

The Gospel of John: Jesus' Teachings
ISBN 1-55945-208-0

Hazardous to Your Health: AIDS, Steroids & Eating Disorders, ISBN 1-55945-200-5

Is Marriage in Your Future?, ISBN 1-55945-203-X

Jesus' Death & Resurrection, ISBN 1-55945-211-0

The Joy of Serving, ISBN 1-55945-210-2

Knowing God's Will, ISBN 1-55945-205-6

Life After High School, ISBN 1-55945-220-X

Making Good Decisions, ISBN 1-55945-209-9

Money: A Christian Perspective, ISBN 1-55945-212-9

Movies, Music, TV & Me, ISBN 1-55945-213-7

Overcoming Insecurities, ISBN 1-55945-221-8

Psalms, ISBN 1-55945-234-X

Real People, Real Faith, ISBN 1-55945-238-2

Responding to Injustice, ISBN 1-55945-214-5

Revelation, ISBN 1-55945-229-3

School Struggles, ISBN 1-55945-201-3

Sex: A Christian Perspective, ISBN 1-55945-206-4

Today's Lessons From Yesterday's Prophets
ISBN 1-55945-227-7

Turning Depression Upside Down, ISBN 1-55945-135-1

What Is the Church?, ISBN 1-55945-222-6

Who Is God?, ISBN 1-55945-218-8

Who Is Jesus?, ISBN 1-55945-219-6

Who Is the Holy Spirit?, ISBN 1-55945-217-X

Your Life as a Disciple, ISBN 1-55945-204-8

Order today from your local Christian bookstore, or write: Group Publishing, Box 485, Loveland, CO 80539.

PUT FAITH INTO ACTION...

...with Group's **Projects With a Purpose™ for Youth Ministry**.

Want to try something different with your 7th—12th grade classes? Group's NEW **Projects With a Purpose™ for Youth Ministry** offers four-week courses that really get kids into their faith. Each **Project With a Purpose** course gives you tools to facilitate a project that will provide a direct, purposeful learning experience. Teenagers will discover something significant about their faith while learning the importance of working together, sharing one another's troubles, and supporting one another in love...plus they'll have lots of fun!

Use for Sunday school classes, midweek meetings, home Bible studies, youth groups, retreats, or any time you want to help teenagers discover more about their faith. Your kids will learn more about each other. They'll practice the life skill of working together. And you'll be rewarded with the knowledge that you're providing a life-changing, faith-building experience for your church's teenagers.

Acting Out Jesus' Parables

Strengthen your teenagers' faith as they are challenged to understand the parables' descriptions of the Christian life. Explore such key issues as the value of humility, the importance of hope, and the relative unimportance of wealth.   ISBN 1-55945-147-5

Celebrating Christ With Youth-Led Worship

Kids love to celebrate. Birthdays. Dating. A new car. For Christians, Jesus is the ultimate reason to celebrate. And as kids celebrate Jesus, they'll grow closer to him—an excitement that will be shared with the whole congregation.   ISBN 1-55945-410-5

Checking Your Church's Pulse

Your teenagers will find new meaning for their faith and build greater appreciation for their church with this course. Interviews with congregational members will help your teenagers, and your church, grow together.   ISBN 1-55945-408-3

Serving Your Neighbors

Strengthen the "service heart" in your teenagers and watch as they discover the joy and value of serving. Your teenagers will appreciate the importance of serving others as they follow Jesus' example.   ISBN 1-55945-406-7

Sharing Your Faith Without Fear

Teenagers don't have to be great orators to share with others what God's love means to them. And teenagers can express their faith through everyday actions and lifestyles without fear of rejection.   ISBN 1-55945-409-1

Teaching Teenagers to Pray

Watch as your teenagers develop strong, effective prayer lives as you introduce them to the basics of prayer. As teenagers explore the depth and excitement of real prayer, they'll learn how to pray with and for others.   ISBN 1-55945-407-5

Teenagers Teaching Children

Teach your teenagers how to share the Gospel with children. Through this course, your teenagers will learn more about their faith by teaching others, and they'll learn lessons about responsibility and develop teaching skills to last a lifetime.   ISBN 1-55945-405-9

Videotaping Your Church Members' Faith Stories

Teenagers will enjoy learning about their congregation—and become players in their church's faith story with this exciting video project. And, they'll learn the depth and power of God's faithfulness to his people.   ISBN 1-55945-239-0

Order today from your local Christian bookstore, or write: Group Publishing, Box 485, Loveland, CO 80539.